Introduction

We would like all our children to be dedicated Bible readers, and the best way to get them started is to give them an early taste of the wonder and excitement contained within the beloved pages of the Bible. To young children, the Bible is a wonderful storybook.

This book has been designed to enable children at the pre-kindergarten to first-grade levels to understand and enjoy a variety of familiar New Testament stories. Each story is written so that it can be easily understood by the children, and suggestions of hand motions, other actions, or visual aids have also been provided to further involve the children.

Sixteen stories are featured, each of which includes either an exciting **activity** reinforcing the story and helping the children develop skills in science, math, or language; or a **fingerplay** that works great as an accompaniment to a particular story or when performed just for fun.

All stories feature simple **questions for discussion** and a fun and stimulating **arts and crafts project** that help the children share the stories at home.

We invite you to use the stories and activities presented in this book to introduce the children to a lifetime of rewarding exploration within the pages of God's own storybook.

Prayer

Jesus, take me by the hand,
Help me learn and understand.
Teach me of God's holy love,
From your heavenly home above.
Dear Friend Jesus, come and stay
Close beside me every day.

Jesus' Birth

(Luke 2:1–20)

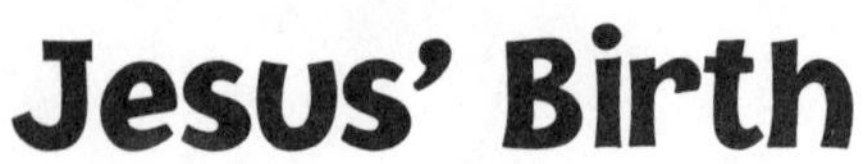

The Night the Angels Sang

(Teach these actions* to accompany the story: donkey—hands to head like ears; baby—cradle and rock arms; shepherds—hand shading eyes, watching sheep; angel—spread arms like wings.)

Mary was going to have a baby* soon. It wasn't a good time for her to take a long trip, but the king said that Mary and Joseph had to go to Bethlehem. Joseph lifted Mary up on the back of a little donkey*, and he led the little animal all the way to Bethlehem.

When Mary and Joseph reached Bethlehem, there was no place for them to stay. A friendly innkeeper said, "I don't have room for you, but you can sleep in my stable if you want to. It's warm and dry, and you can keep your donkey* there with the rest of the animals.

So that's where Mary and Joseph were that night, when their baby* was born. Mary remembered what the angel* had told her about her baby* son: he would be the Savior, the Son of God, and she should name him Jesus. She carefully wrapped the baby* in a blanket and laid him in a manger filled with sweet-smelling hay.

In the fields outside of Bethlehem, there were flocks of sheep, and there were shepherds* watching over them. It was dark and quiet in the fields. Then suddenly, the sky was bright with a great light, and an angel* appeared. "I'm bringing you good news from God!" said the angel*. "Tonight, the Savior has been born in Bethlehem. To find him, go into town and find a stable. There is a baby* there, wrapped in a blanket, lying in a manger."

The shepherds* rushed into town. There they found the stable. And just as the angel* had told them, there was the baby* called Jesus, lying in the manger. There was Mary and Joseph, and there was the little donkey*. The shepherds* knelt down and thanked God for sending them their Savior. And up in the sky, a whole choir of angels* sang: "Glory to God in the highest—and peace on earth!"

 GP275102 New Testament

Jesus' Birth

(Fingerplay)

Let's Talk About the Story

- Where did Mary and Joseph have to stay? *(in a stable)*
- What did Mary use as a bed for baby Jesus? *(a manger)*
- Where did the angel tell the shepherds to go? *(Bethlehem)*
- What song did the angels sing? *("Glory to God in the highest!")*

Bethlehem Fingerplay

(Use the gestures shown
for each underlined word.)

Down in little Bethlehem,
A holy baby came.
Mary laid him in the straw,
And Jesus was his name.

Up above the hillside,
The herald angels fly,
And Mary rocks her baby,
And sings a lullaby.

Up in the heavens,
A star is shining bright,
And little baby Jesus
Is sleeping in the night.

Down in the stable,
The wise men bring their gold,
And Mary wraps her baby up
To keep him from the cold.

Down in little Bethlehem,
A holy baby came.
Mary laid him in the straw,
And Jesus was his name.

     GP275102 New Testament

Jesus' Birth

(Craft Page)

The Flying Angel

This happy Christmas angel can be decorated with bright colors and fly on the end of a string!

Materials needed: photocopies of this craft page, crayons, scissors, glue, tape, string

Directions: Have the children color and cut out the patterns on the bold lines. Show them how to roll the angels and glue as shown. Then they can glue the wing tabs to the bodies. Tape a 10" length of string to each angel head and tie a loop on the opposite end.

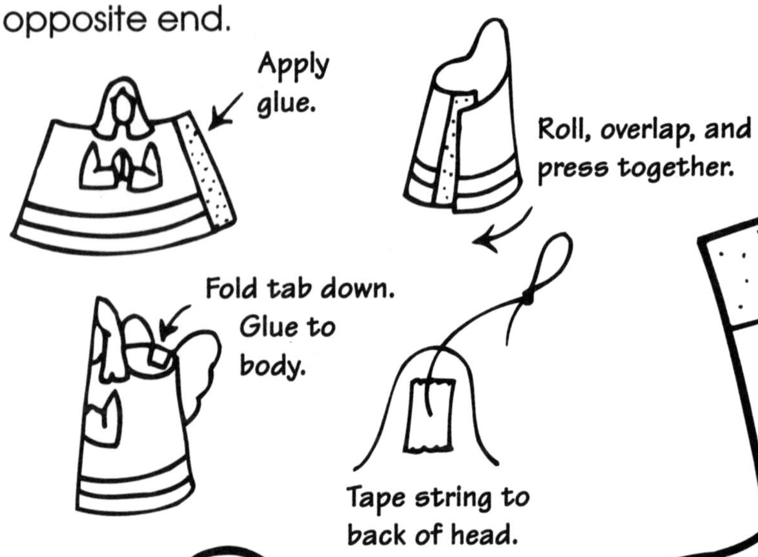

GP275102 New Testament

The Wise Men

(Matthew 2:1-12)

The Big Beautiful Star

(Use the star pattern on page 7 to make a hanging visual aid for this story.)

When Jesus was born in Bethlehem, a wicked king was ruling the country. His name was King Herod.

At the same time, there were three wise men who lived in other countries far away. Each of the wise men was very excited by something they had seen in the sky—a big, beautiful star. It was the biggest star they had ever seen, and it shone more brightly than any other star in the sky. All of the wise men decided that it must mean something special.

So the three men started traveling toward the big star, and they began talking about the star. They finally figured out that it must mean that someone important had been born: the Savior that the Jewish people had been waiting for for so long.

The wise men thought that the king of the country should know where to find the newborn baby, so they went to King Herod. "Where is the baby?" they asked. "Where is the Savior, the King of the Jews?"

King Herod was frightened to think that there was a new king in his country! He asked his advisers where the baby might be. They said, "The prophets said he would be born in Bethlehem."

Herod told the wise men: "Go and find the baby. Then come and tell me where he is. I want to go and worship him, too." But Herod really meant to kill this King of the Jews!

The wise men followed the big beautiful star to the stable in Bethlehem. There they found Mary and Joseph and baby Jesus. "We have come to see the Savior!" said the wise men. They laid down their gifts—gold, frankincense, and myrrh—by the little manger. They had found the wonderful baby, God's own Son.

And what do you think the wise men did then? They went right back home. They didn't go back and tell King Herod where the baby was because they knew Herod might hurt him. And for the rest of their lives, they remembered that big, beautiful star!

   GP275102 New Testament

The Wise Men
(Activity Page)

Let's Talk About the Story

- What did the wise men think when they saw the star? *(They thought it meant that someone special had been born.)*
- What did the wise men ask King Herod? *(Where is the King of the Jews?)*
- Did Herod really want to go and worship the baby? *(No. He wanted to kill him.)*
- What did the wise men do when they found Jesus? *(They gave him gifts.)*
- Where did the wise men go after they left Bethlehem? *(home)*

Smell-Good Gifts

Ahead of time, make up small netting bags of potpourri for each child. Tie a 30"-loop of yarn to each. Prepare a collection of gold-colored objects and things that smell good (bay leaves, incense, flowers, cinnamon, pine branch, perfume, soap).

In class, remind the children that the wise men brought gifts of gold, myrrh, and frankincense to the stable. Ask what they think these gifts were like. Show the children the gold objects. Then explain that the other gifts were things that smelled good. Pass around a bay leaf, newly broken, and say that the myrrh probably smelled something like that. Pass around the incense, identifying it as frankincense, similar to what the wise men brought.

Let the children handle and name the other smell-good things in your collection and comment that things that smell good are all gifts from God. Hang a potpourri bag around the neck of each child.

    GP275102 New Testament

The Wise Men

(Craft Page)

The Big Beautiful Star

The children will enjoy decorating this star the wise men followed and finding a place to hang it up at home.

Materials needed: photocopies of this craft page, crayons, several colors of curly ribbon, scissors, tape

Directions: Let the children decorate their stars and cut them out along the bold lines. Cut six 12"-ribbons for each star and tape these ribbons to the back of each star. Tape one 10"-length of ribbon to the top point of each star and tie a loop in the other end.

Back View

Jesus in the Temple

(Luke 2:41–52)

Where Are You, Jesus?

(You might use the craft on page 10 to illustrate this story.)

When Jesus was twelve years old, his parents took him on a long trip. Jesus was very excited! They were going to Jerusalem, that big city where the temple stood *(show children the temple with the door closed)*. They were going there to celebrate the Feast of the Passover.

Many other friends and family members would be traveling on the road to Jerusalem, too. It would take many days to get there, but nobody minded; they would be talking and singing and having a good time along the way. Sometimes Jesus would walk with other people for awhile and then come back and join his parents.

After the long journey, the group entered through the gates of the city. Everywhere, there were happy crowds—in the streets, in the inns and houses, and in the big temple. Inside the temple, priests were leading the people in worship. Wise old men sat talking together about God and how to live a good life. And all the time, Jesus was looking and listening and learning.

At the end of the Passover celebration, everyone packed up and started home. Mary and Joseph had walked a long way when Mary said, "Where is Jesus? I thought he was walking with our relatives, but nobody seems to know where he is." The worried parents asked everyone if they had seen Jesus. But nobody had seen him since they left Jerusalem!

Mary and Joseph turned around and hurried back to the city. They looked and looked for Jesus, in the streets and inns and houses. Last of all, they went to the temple. There he was *(open the temple door)* talking to the wise old men about God.

"We've been so worried about you!" said Mary. "We've been looking everywhere!"

Jesus was sorry that they were worried, but he said quietly, "Didn't you know that I would be here in the temple, in my Father's house?" Mary and Joseph didn't quite understand what he meant, but we know, don't we? Jesus knew he was the Son of God, and that he was in God's house, the temple. All the way back home, Mary kept thinking about what Jesus had said.

GP275102 New Testament

Jesus in the Temple

(Activity Page)

Let's Talk About the Story

- Why was Jesus' family going to Jerusalem? *(to celebrate the Feast of the Passover)*
- What was happening inside the temple? *(Priests were leading worship; wise men were talking about God.)*
- On the way back home, what did Mary and Joseph discover? *(that Jesus was missing)*
- Where did Mary and Joseph find Jesus? *(in the temple)*
- Why did Jesus call the temple his Father's house? *(He knew he was the Son of God.)*

Find the Lost Boy

Ahead of class time, photocopy and cut out the game pieces below. Tell the children that when Jesus' parents thought he was lost, they found him in the temple. Play a game called "Find the Lost Boy" (similar to charades). One by one, give each child a game piece and whisper to him or her where the lost boy is. The child must give clues to the class without talking. The class gets three guesses. Then the child can tell where the lost boy is.

Behind a tree

In a car

In a house

Under a table

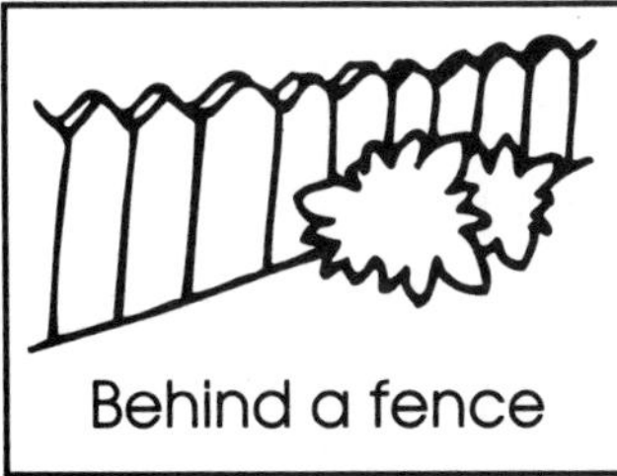

Behind a fence

In a bathtub

Behind a door

Behind a chair

Under a bed

Under a rug

In an airplane

In a boat

    GP275102 New Testament

# Jesus in the Temple

(Craft Page)

Jesus in the Temple

The children can use this craft to retell the story at home. Where is Jesus? Open the temple door and find out!

Materials needed: photocopies of this craft page, crayons, scissors, glue

Directions: Have the children color the two parts of the craft and cut along the bold lines. Help them glue the picture of Jesus inside the temple as shown.

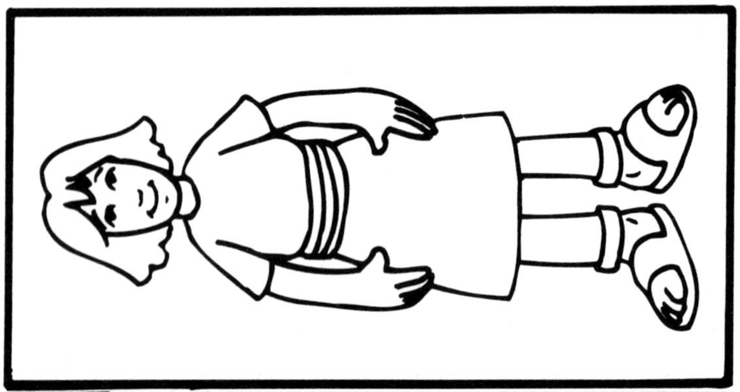

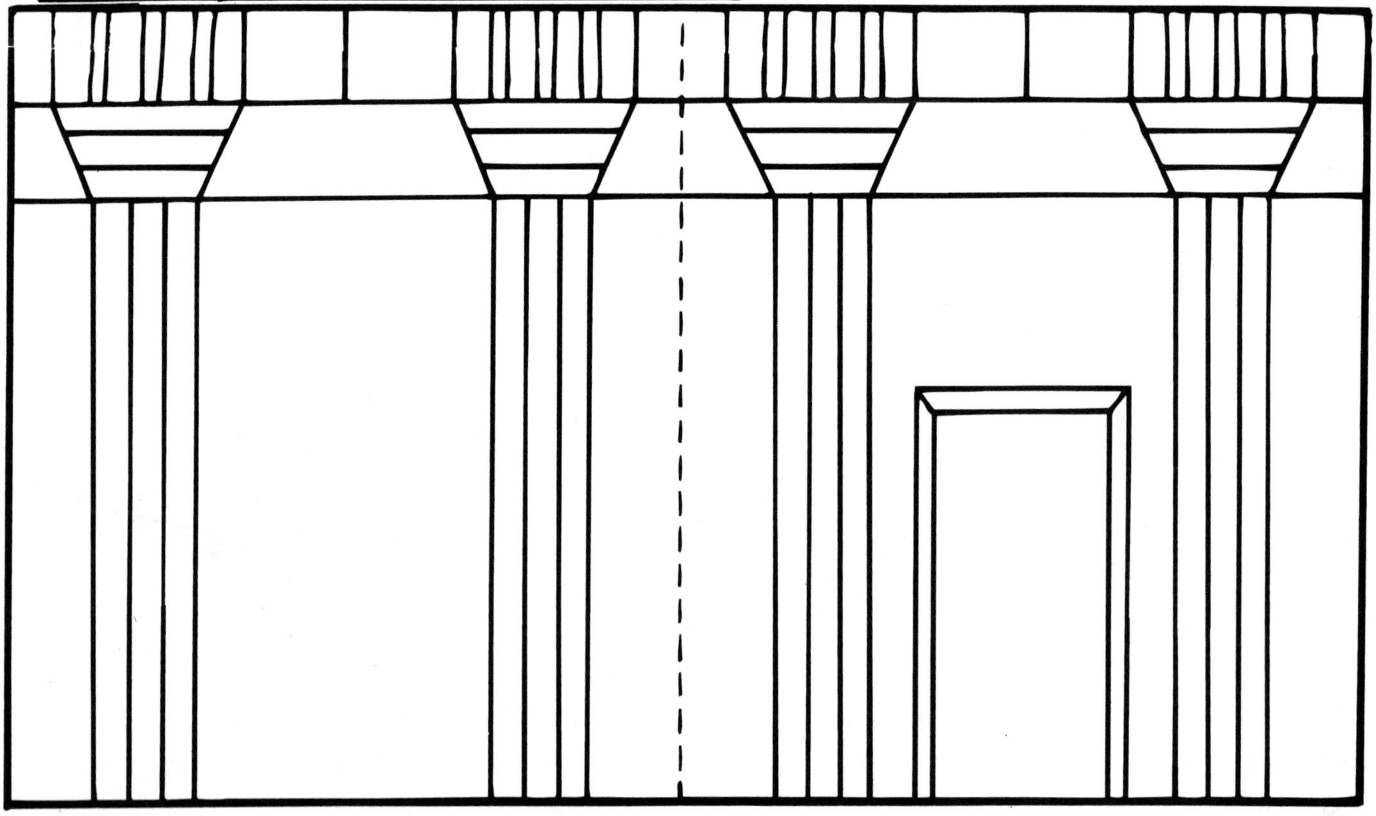

GP275102 New Testament

Peter

(Luke 5:1–11, Matthew 16:13–20)

Simon Gets a New Name

(You might complete the craft on page 13 and hang it up while you tell this story.)

When Jesus first started preaching to people about God's love, he was all alone. Now, trying to tell everyone the Good News was a big job, and he knew he couldn't do it all alone. So he began to look for friends to help him.

One day, when Jesus was walking near a lake, he saw a fishing boat out on the water. On board was a big, strong man, a fisherman called Simon. He and his brother were throwing nets over the side of the boat to catch fish. Jesus watched for a while, and then he called, "Come with me, and I'll teach you a different kind of fishing!"

Simon thought, "What could I fish for besides fish?" He steered his boat closer to shore.

"I will make you fishers of people," said Jesus. "Together, we can bring people to God as you bring your fish into your boat."

Simon knew about Jesus. People said that Jesus was the Savior that the people of Israel had been waiting for. Jesus called himself the Son of God, and Simon believed him. "I will come and help you fish for people!" Simon said.

After Simon had been with Jesus for a long time, Jesus asked him, "Who do you think I am?"

Simon answered right away: "You're the Savior, the Messiah, the Son of God."

"Good for you!" Jesus said. "You are a good, strong man, and you understand what I have been saying. I choose you to start my church. And because you're strong and brave and loyal, I'm going to give you a new name: Peter, a name which means 'Rock.' Now you're not Simon the Fisherman anymore. You're Peter the Fisherman, the fisher of people."

Many years later, when Jesus was gone from the earth, Peter kept on traveling and preaching, just as he had with his friend Jesus. And now and then, when he was tired and afraid, Peter would think about the name Jesus had given him. "I'm not afraid," Peter would say. "I am Peter the Fisherman. I am Peter the Rock."

  GP275102 New Testament

Peter

(Fingerplay)

Let's Talk About the Story

- Why was Jesus looking for friends to help him? *(Preaching the Good News was a big job.)*

- Where did Jesus find Simon? *(on a fishing boat)*

- What did Jesus want to make Simon? *(a fisherman of people)*

- What new name did Jesus give Simon? *(Peter)*

One Little Fishy Fingerplay

(Use the gestures shown for each underlined word. Just for fun, repeat the fingerplay, speeding up the action!)

<u>One</u> little fishy, in the ocean blue.
Another <u>swam</u> along, and then there were <u>two</u>.

<u>Two</u> little fishies, swimming in the sea.
Another <u>swam</u> along, and then there were <u>three</u>.

<u>Three</u> little fishies, swimming more and more.
Another <u>swam</u> along, and then there were <u>four</u>.

<u>Four</u> little fishies, loved to swim and dive.
Another <u>swam</u> along, and then there were <u>five</u>.

<u>Five</u> little fishies, swimming in the bay.
Along came a storm, and they all <u>swam away</u>!

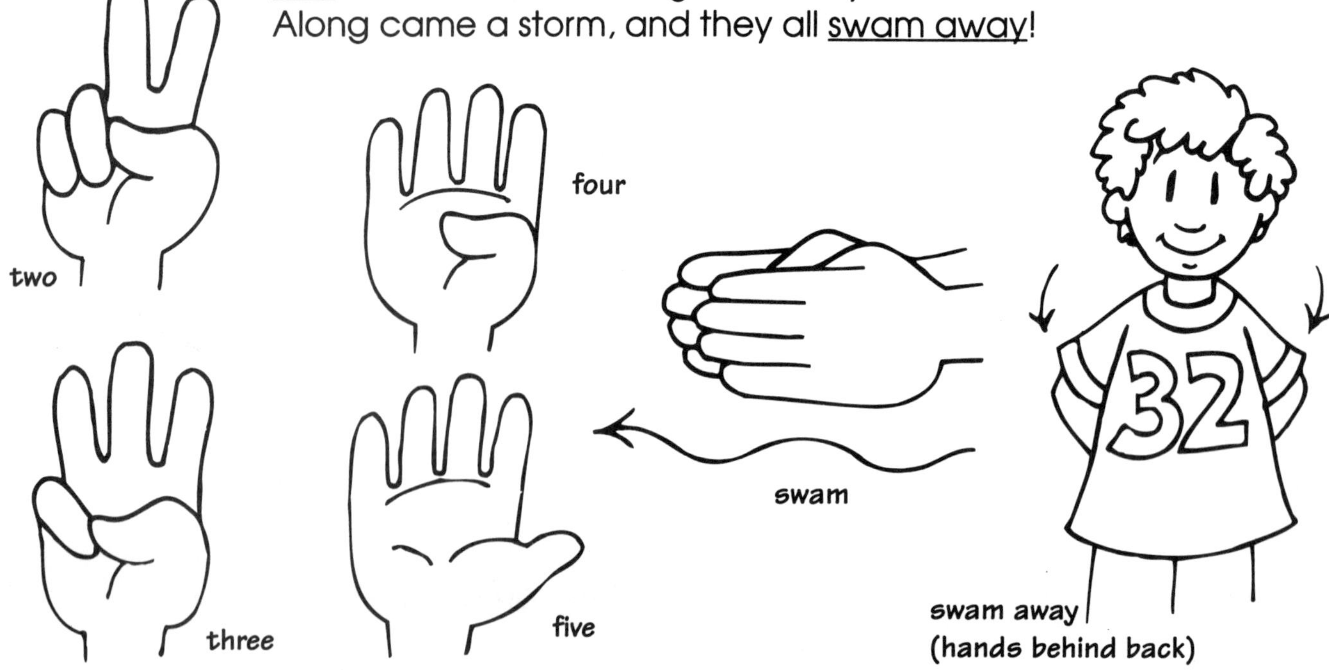

GP275102 New Testament

Peter

(Craft Page)

A Fish Kite

This craft celebrates the new name of Peter that Jesus gave to Simon the fisherman. Watch it fly in the wind!

Materials needed: photocopies of this craft page, crayons, scissors, ribbon or streamers, tape, hole punch, string

Directions: Have the children color their fish and cut them out along the bold lines. Cut 6–8 streamers or ribbons into 15" lengths for each fish and help the children tape them to the tails of their fish as shown. Punch a hole in each nose and tie a 16"-length of string in the hole. Tape the holes to prevent tearing.

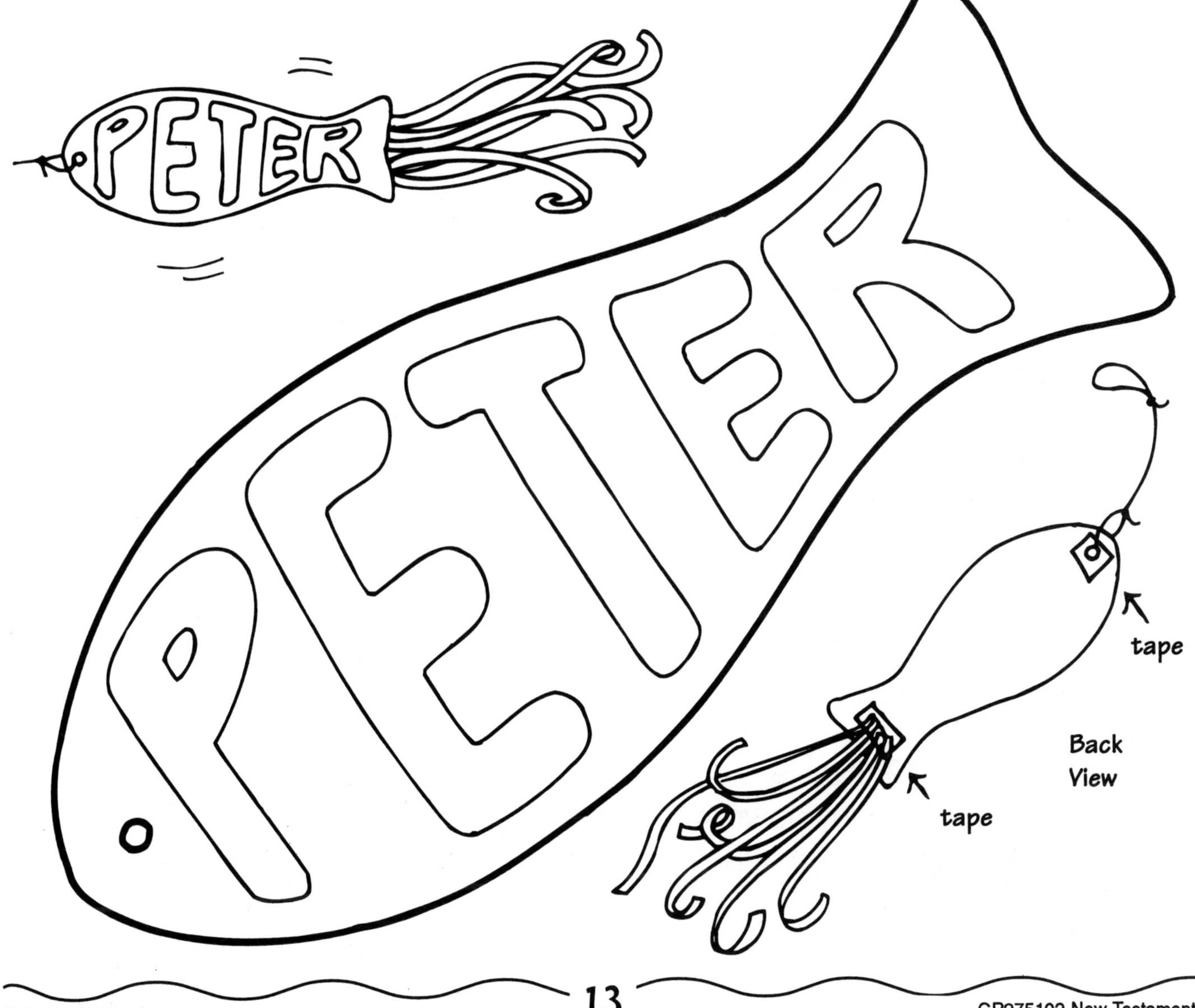

GP275102 New Testament

Jesus Calms the Storm

(Mark 4:35–41)

Jesus Stops the Storm

(You might use the craft on page 16 to illustrate this story.)

One day, Jesus was preaching by a lake. When he was tired, he decided to get into a boat and go to the other side of the lake.

Jesus' friends began to row the boat while Jesus slept. Suddenly, a storm came up. A strong wind blew and a heavy rain fell, and the waves grew higher and higher. They rocked the boat back and forth and up and down—just a little at first, and then more and more. The frightened men in the boat hung on for dear life! They were sure the boat was going to tip over and they would drown in the wild, dark ocean.

But all the time the wind was blowing and the boat was rocking, Jesus lay peacefully asleep in the back of the boat. Finally, the men couldn't stand it anymore. They woke Jesus up. "The boat is going to tip over, and we're all going to drown!" they said. "Don't you care that your friends are in danger?"

Jesus looked at his friends and said, "Why are you so scared? Don't you know that nothing bad can happen as long as you're with me?" And then he stood up in the rocking boat, and he held out his hands. He said: "Be quiet, sea! Stop blowing, wind!" Right away, the wind stopped blowing, the waves grew small and peaceful, and the boat stopped rocking.

Then Jesus went and lay down in the back of the boat again. In the stillness of the night, one of the men asked, "Who is this man who can tame the wind and the waves?"

Another man whispered softly, "He really is the Son of God!"

  GP275102 New Testament

Jesus Calms the Storm

(Activity Page)

Let's Talk About the Story

- Why did Jesus get in the boat? *(He was tired and wanted to go to the other side of the lake.)*

- What did Jesus do when he got in the boat? *(He went to sleep.)*

- What happened to frighten the men? *(A storm came up.)*

- What did Jesus do when he woke up? *(He calmed the storm.)*

- What did the men think of Jesus then? *(that he truly was the Son of God)*

Let's Take a Boat Trip

Tell the children that they are going to take a boat trip like the one Jesus and his friends took. Ask them to place some chairs in a circle to represent the boat. Then sit on the floor inside the circle. As you narrate, encourage the children to make the appropriate movements and sounds as indicated in the story.

Is everyone on board our little boat? Then here we go—out to sea! Can you feel the boat rocking? Let's rock back and forth, back and forth, on the waves of the sea. Can you see how bright the sun is? *(Look up at the sky and point to the sun.)* Can you see the big fish, jumping out of the water? *(Look at the water and point to the fish.)* How big are the fish? Show me with your hands.

We're rocking and rocking on the nice bright sea. *(Keep rocking.)* Oh-oh! I think I see a cloud in the sky. *(Look up at the sky.)* Do you see that big black cloud? I think I see another one, and another one. I feel raindrops falling on our heads! *(Cover up your head.)*

The rain is falling harder! The wind is blowing! *(Make a sound like the wind.)* The boat is rocking more and more—way over to this side, and way over to the other! *(Keep rocking.)* This is getting scary!

Let's wake up Jesus and ask him to help us. Let's all say, "Wake up, Jesus!" Jesus is standing up in the boat. He's holding out his hands and saying, "Be quiet, sea and wind!" Look! The boat isn't rocking anymore. *(Stop rocking.)* What do we say to Jesus for saving us from the storm?

    GP275102 New Testament

Jesus Calms the Storm

(Craft Page)

The Boat in the Storm

It's a very small boat, and a very stormy sea! When this craft is completed, the little vessel will rock on the big waves.

Materials needed: photocopies of this craft page, crayons, scissors, paper punch, brass paper tacks

Directions: Let the children color the boat and sea. Then they can cut them out along the bold lines. Fold the seas on the dotted lines and punch a hole through both layers. Punch a hole in the boats, and insert each boat into the sea, matching holes. Secure with paper tacks.

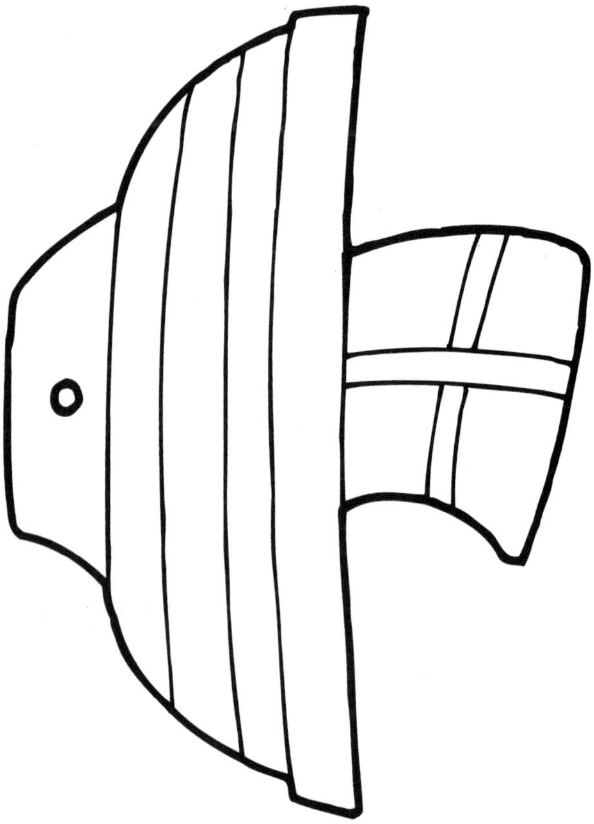

GP275102 New Testament

Jesus Feeds the Multitude

(Mark 8:1–13)

Food, Food, and More Food!

(You might bring in a piece of pita bread and ask the children this question: "Is this enough for one person, or for everybody?" At the appropriate moment in the story*, divide the bread among the children. Willingness to share is the secret of this story!)

A big crowd of people had come out into the country to hear Jesus preach. They listened to him talk about God's love for them.

When it began growing late, Jesus turned to his friends and said, "I feel sorry for these people. They've been with me a long time, and they're all getting hungry. We ought to feed them."

Jesus' friends said, "There are hundreds of people here. How could we feed such a big crowd?"

Jesus asked them, "How many loaves of bread do we have?"

His friends answered, "Only seven. We have a few fish, too, but that's not nearly enough food for everyone."

"Well," said Jesus, "Let's share what we have. If we share, God is sure to take care of us all."

So Jesus blessed the bread and fish, and his friends passed them out to the crowd.* Everybody took some. And then a strange thing happened— they saw that everyone had plenty to eat. There was still enough to feed the whole big crowd! When all the people had finished eating, they collected what was left, and guess what? There were seven baskets of food left over!

Jesus and his friends and the people must have been thinking that God makes wonderful things happen when we share!

Jesus Feeds the Multitude

(Activity Page)

Let's Talk About the Story

- Why did Jesus feel sorry for the people? *(He knew they were hungry.)*

- How many loaves of bread did they have? *(seven)*

- What did Jesus tell his friends to do with the food? *(share it)*

- What happened when the food was passed out to the crowd? *(There was plenty for everyone.)*

- How much food was left over after the people had eaten? *(seven baskets)*

Let's Share a Snack

Give each child a plastic knife and a paper plate containing apple slices, other fruit, and a small mound of peanut butter. As the children spread peanut butter on their apple slices or other fruit, remind them that all food (even the peanuts in the peanut butter) comes to us from God.

 GP275102 New Testament

Jesus Feeds the Multitude

(Craft Page)

A Basketful of Food

The children will enjoy making and showing this miraculous basket of food. One little bite unfolds to become many!

Materials needed: photocopies of this craft page, crayons, scissors, tape

Directions: Let the children color their baskets and food pictures and cut them out along the bold lines. Then they fold their baskets on the dotted lines and tape as shown. The children can accordion-fold the food pictures and insert them into their baskets.

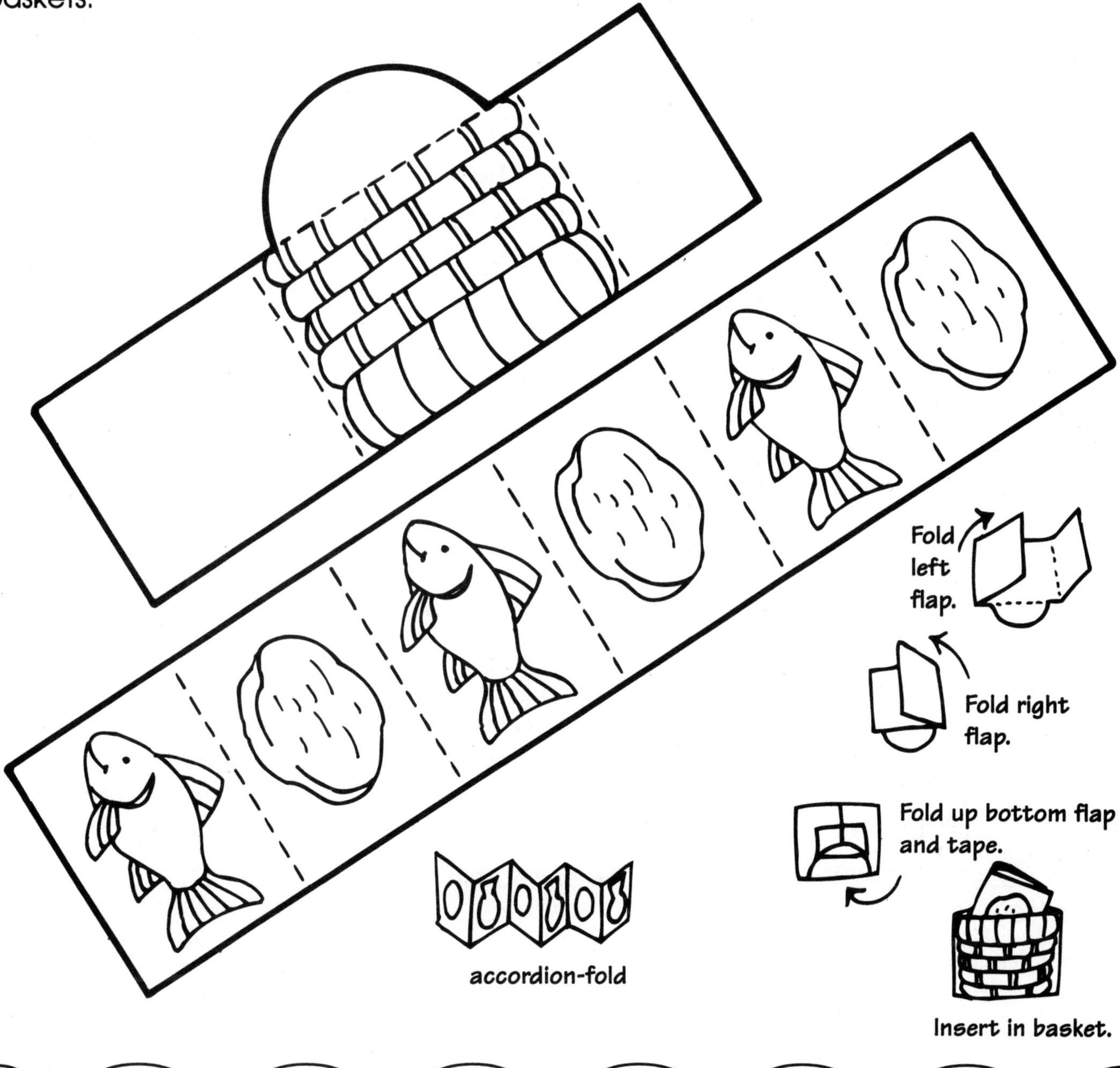

The Good Samaritan

(Luke 10:25–37)

A Helping Hand

(Lead the children in using these hand actions to tell this story: *men's footsteps/walking—pat knees; *horse's hoofbeats—pat left, pat right, clap hands; *donkey—repeat horse sound, more quickly.)

Jesus liked to tell stories to teach people how they could live a good life. Once, he told this story about the Good Samaritan:

A man was walking* along a road all by himself, traveling from Jericho to Jerusalem. Suddenly, several robbers jumped out from behind some rocks. They attacked the poor traveler and took his clothes and money. They left him hurt, lying by the road.

The hurt man could only lie there and hope that someone would come and help him. After a long time, he heard the sound of footsteps*. He saw a tall, dignified-looking man coming down the road. "Help me!" cried the traveler. "I need a helping hand!"

But the tall man was scared. "If I stop to help, the robbers will come and get me!" he said, and he hurried away.

The hurt man waited and waited, and after a while, he heard the sound of a horse's hoofbeats* coming toward him down the road. A man with a big beard was sitting in the saddle. "Help me!" cried the hurt man. "I need a helping hand!"

But the bearded man didn't even get off his horse. "If I stop to help you, I'll be late!" he said. The hurt man heard the hoofbeats* grow quieter and quieter as the bearded man rode off down the road.

The hurt man had almost given up when a good man, a Samaritan, came riding down the road on his donkey*. "Help me!" cried the hurt man. "I need a helping hand!" Right away, the Good Samaritan got down off his donkey. He gave the hurt man a drink of cool water and bandaged his wounds. Then he put the hurt man on the back of the donkey* and took him to an inn where he could rest and get better.

After Jesus had told this story, someone asked him, "Should I give a helping hand to everybody?"

I think Jesus must have said, "Everybody needs a helping hand sometimes." *(Have children hold up both hands.)* All of us need to have helping hands, just like the Good Samaritan!

The Good Samaritan

(Activity Page)

Let's Talk About the Story

- What happened to the man traveling to Jericho? *(He was attacked by robbers.)*

- Why didn't the first man help the hurt man? *(He was afraid the robbers would attack him, too.)*

- Why didn't the second man help the hurt man? *(He didn't want to be late.)*

- Are those good excuses for not helping? *(No.)*

- What did the Good Samaritan do? *(gave him water, bandaged him, took him to an inn)*

Helping Hands Bulletin Board

Ahead of class time, use a 6"-diameter saucer as a pattern to cut circles (representing balloons) from several bright colors of construction paper. In class, trace around each child's hand on white paper and print his or her name on it. Cut out the hands. Glue each hand on a construction paper circle. Punch a hole at the bottom and attach a piece of yarn. Display as shown.

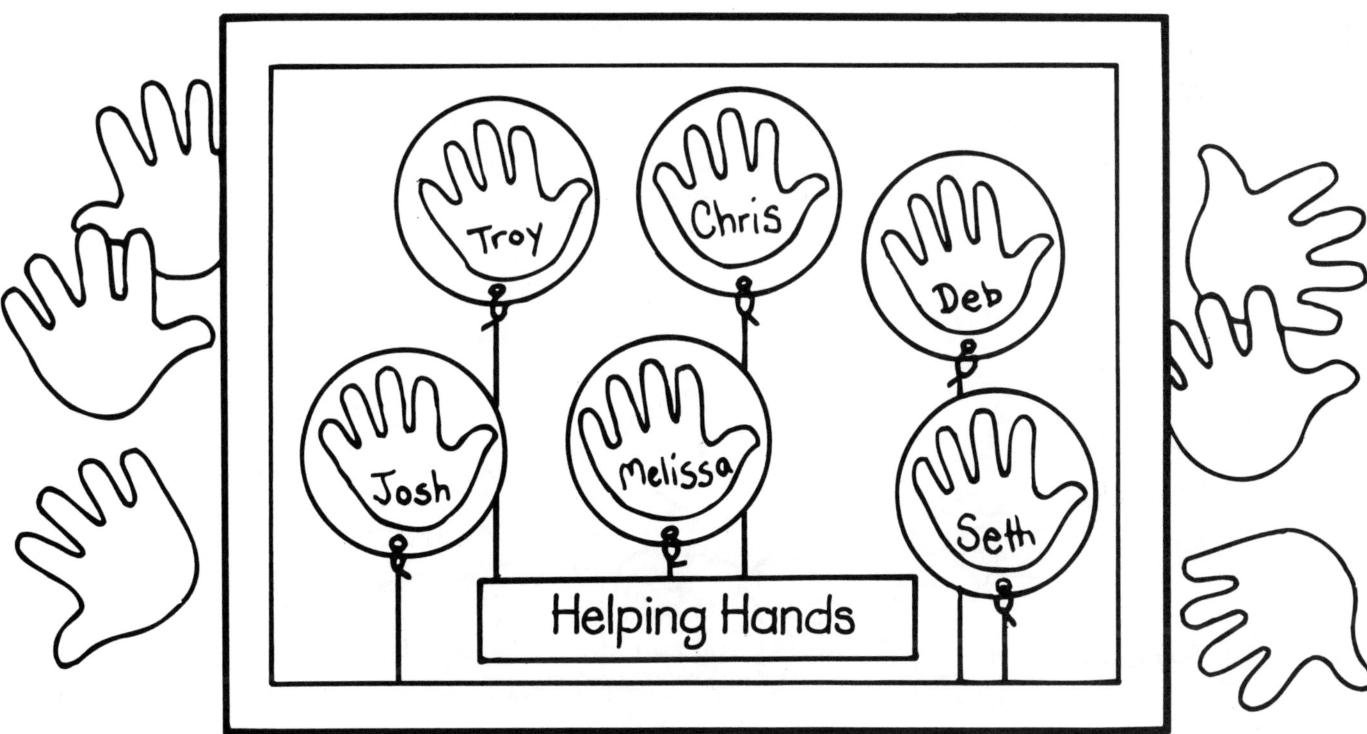

GP275102 New Testament

The Good Samaritan

(Craft Page)

A Helping Hand Reminder

This little reminder might stand on the family dinner table at home to inspire some helpful deeds.

Materials needed: photocopies of this craft page, crayons, scissors, glue

Directions: Have the children color the pattern and cut it out along the bold lines. Roll and glue as shown.

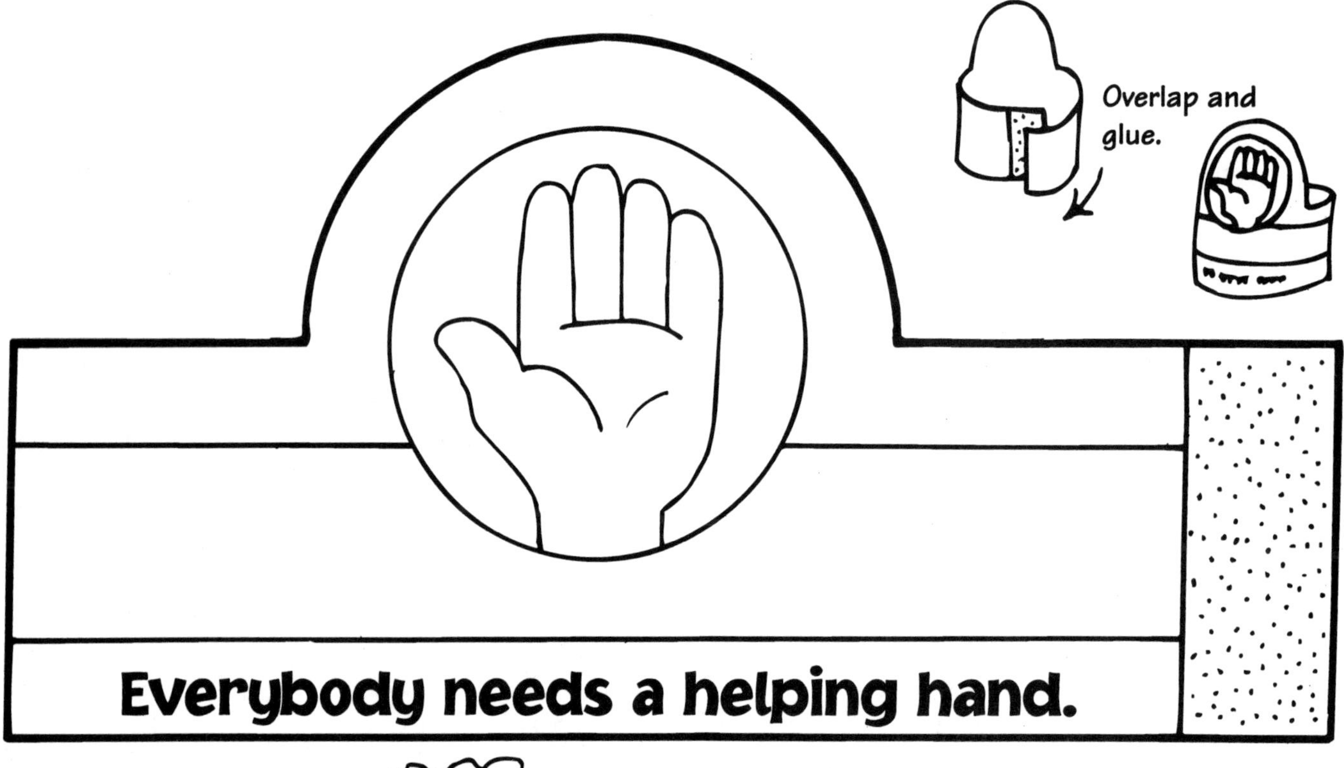

 GP275102 New Testament

The Parable of the Lost Sheep

(Matthew 18:10–14)

Ninety-Nine Sheep Plus One

(You might use the craft sheep on page 25 to illustrate this story.)

Jesus liked to tell people how much God loved them. He said, "No matter how many people there are on earth, every single person is important to God." To help the people understand, Jesus told this story about a shepherd and his sheep:

Once there was a shepherd who owned 100 sheep. When he took them out into the fields in the morning, he counted every one. When he brought them back at night, he counted them again. He wanted to make sure that all 100 of them were safe.

But one night, he counted only 99 sheep. Just to make sure there was no mistake, he counted them again. Yes, there were only 99. One sheep was missing!

Even though it was getting dark, the shepherd started out into the fields to look for his lost sheep. There were so many bad things that could happen to a little sheep that was lost and alone. Wolves and bears were lurking in the dark. There were deep holes and rivers that a little animal might fall into. The shepherd walked and walked and called and called.

Suddenly, way off in the distance, he heard the sound of a tiny voice: "Baa! Baa! Baa!" it cried. He hurried toward the sound, and the voice got louder and clearer as he ran. He stopped and listened, and then looked down. There was the sad little sheep, down at the bottom of a deep hole where it had fallen.

The shepherd was so happy! He spoke softly to the sheep as he lifted it out of the hole. He carried it gently in his arms all the way back home.

The shepherd was so glad to have that one sheep safe and sound that he gave a party and invited his friends to celebrate. He knew his friends must think he was a little silly to worry about one small sheep when he had 99 more. But he didn't care. He just knew that every single one was important to him—just as every single one of you is important to God.

GP275102 New Testament

The Parable of the Lost Sheep

(Activity Page)

Let's Talk About the Story

- How many sheep did the shepherd have? *(100)*
- What did the shepherd do every morning and night? *(He counted his sheep.)*
- Why was the shepherd worried about his lost sheep? *(There were wild animals in the fields and dangerous holes and rivers.)*
- Where did the shepherd find the lost sheep? *(in a deep hole)*
- What did the shepherd do to celebrate? *(He gave a party.)*
- What does the story tell us about God's love? *(Each one of us is important to God.)*

Let's Act Out the Story

Ahead of time, photocopy a pair of sheep ears for each child using the patterns below. Staple each pair onto a 2" x 22" construction paper strip. Fit them to each child's head and staple. Choose one child to be the shepherd and let the rest be sheep. Tell the story and let the children act it out. (It's fun to do this outdoors if weather permits.)

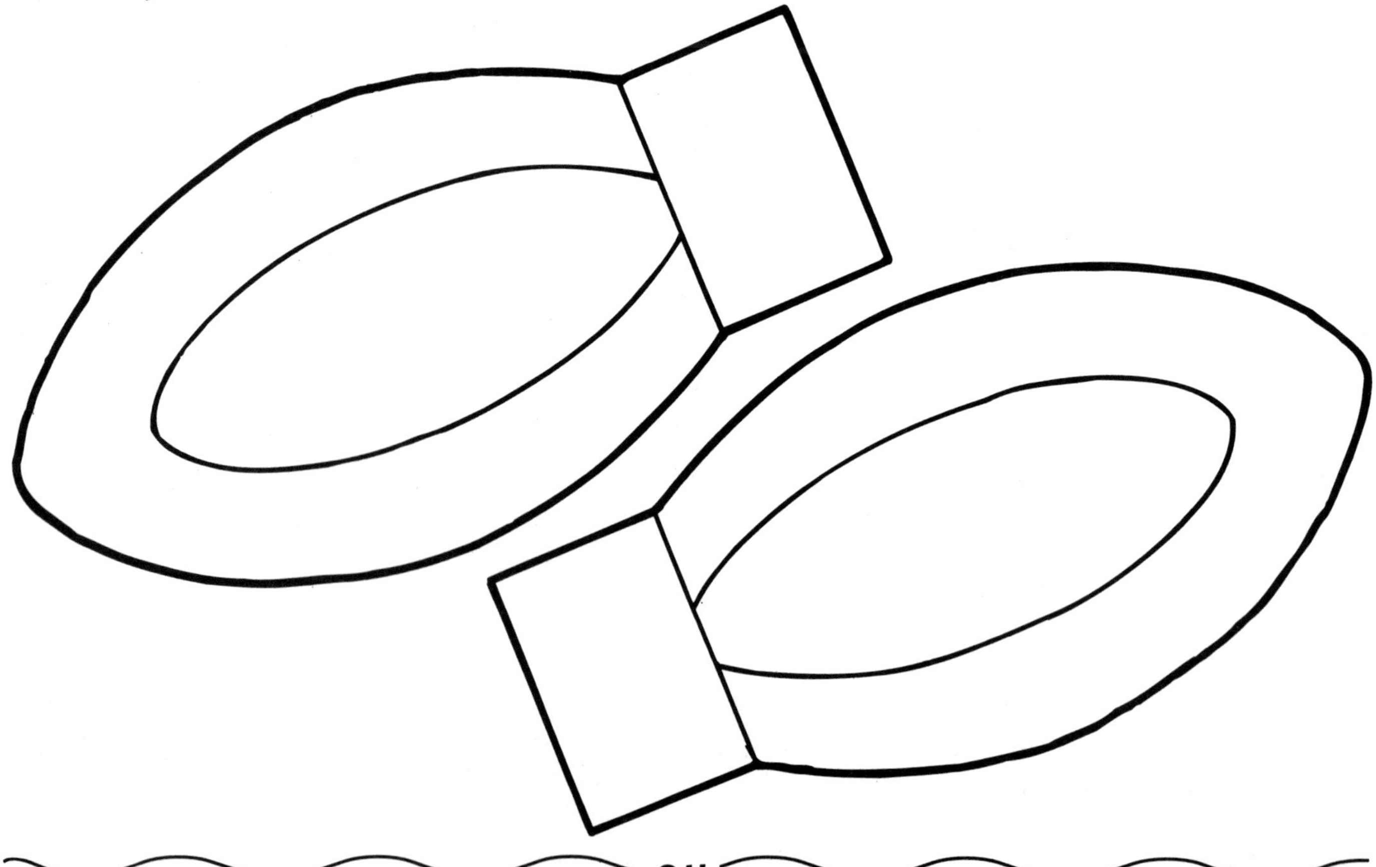

The Parable of the Lost Sheep

(Craft Page)

The Little Lost Sheep

When all the sheep are finished, you might gather them together on a tabletop to count them, just as the shepherd did!

Materials needed: photocopies of this craft page, gummed reinforcements, scissors, glue

Directions: Let the children place gummed reinforcements (overlapping) all over the back and sides of their sheep. Then they cut out their sheep along the bold lines, fold on the dotted lines, and glue as shown.

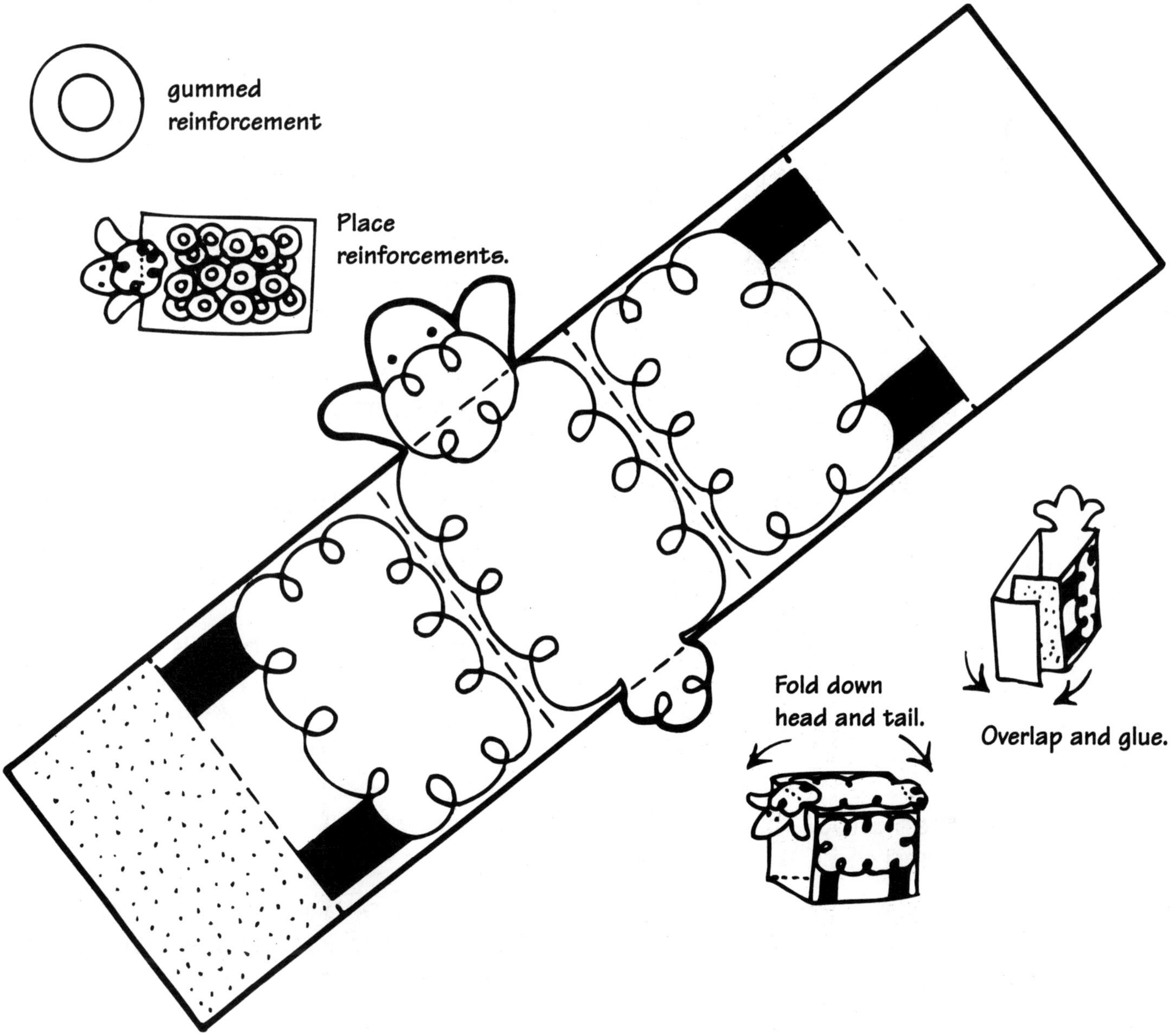

GP275102 New Testament

The Prodigal Son

(Luke 15:1–7)

Fresh-Start Words

(You might use the craft on page 28 to accompany this story, pulling out the sun at the appropriate moment*.)

Jesus wanted people to know that God would give them a fresh start after they had done something wrong. There are secret words that can be used when someone needs a fresh start. Can you guess what they are? You'll hear about them in one of Jesus' stories.

A wealthy farmer had a son who worked for him on his land. The young man came to his father one day and said, "I'm tired of working for you. I want to go out and see the world and have some fun. I know you've saved up some money for me. Let me have it now, so I can go and find work somewhere else."

That made the father very sad, but he thought that the son had a right to find a different job if he wanted to. So he gave his son the money. The father watched as the young man walked away from him, down the road, and disappeared around the bend.

The son walked a long time until he came to a big city. Since he had plenty of money, he didn't bother looking for a job. He just spent it having fun. He found some new friends, and they treated him very well. He had plenty of money for fun and parties and presents.

One day, the young man reached into his pocket and found that his money was all gone! Then his friends weren't so kind to him anymore. They had only liked him when he had a lot of money to spend. Now he had to get a job. But the only job he could find was taking care of someone's pigs. He felt lonely and homesick, and he was so hungry that even the pigs' food began to look good to him. One day, he thought, "I've been a foolish son and treated my father badly. I'm going to go home right now and see if I can make things right."

A few days later, the father looked out of the window and saw his son coming back. He ran out to meet him. The minute he saw his father, the son said two of the secret words: * "I'm sorry." His father then said three more secret words: "I forgive you." These are good words to use when you need a fresh start!

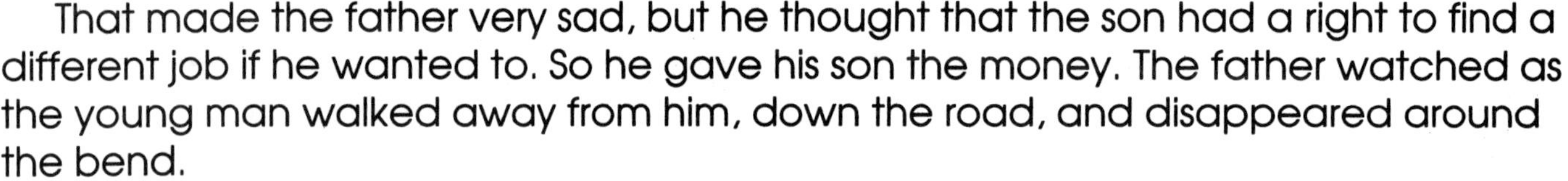

The Prodigal Son
(Activity Page)

Let's Talk About the Story

- How did the father feel when his son went away? *(sad)*
- What job did the son find for himself after his money was gone? *(feeding pigs)*
- What secret words did the son say when he came back? *("I'm sorry.")*
- What secret words did the father say? *("I forgive you.")*

A Good Words Scroll

Ahead of time, make a photocopy of the scroll below for each child. Roll each one up and tie it with a ribbon. Show the children a copy of the scroll and talk about the useful words on it. Talk about when we might want to use them. Give the children the scrolls to take home.

The Prodigal Son

(Craft Page)

Fresh-Start Rising Sun

Just when things are going wrong, this sun, with its fresh-start words, can be pulled out to brighten things up!

Materials needed: photocopies of this craft page, crayons, scissors, glue

Directions: Let the children color the two parts and cut them out along the bold lines. Then they fold on the dotted lines and glue as shown. Show them how to insert their suns in the pockets.

GP275102 New Testament

The Little Children and Jesus

(Mark 10:13–16)

Children Are Special

(The words in parentheses invite the children to follow your actions as you tell the story.)

When Jesus preached, a lot of grown-up people used to come and listen. They'd listen and learn and talk to him about God. They knew he had important things to tell them. Sometimes they brought their children along to listen, too, even though they thought the children wouldn't understand.

One day, there were a great many children in the crowd around Jesus. Many of them were thinking what a kind man Jesus was. So the ones on the far edges of the crowd stood up. *(Stand up two fingers on each leg and walk them forward.)* They began to come closer. They took their mothers and fathers by the hand, and they said, "Let's go even closer to Jesus."

The children took a few more steps, and a few more, and a few more, until they were right up in front where they could look into Jesus' face and hear every word he said. The children smiled at him, and the parents smiled at him. "Please bless our children!" said the mothers and fathers. "Put your hands on their heads and bless them!"

But Jesus' friends didn't like all the children crowding around him. They thought Jesus was too important to pay any attention to children. They tried to shoo the children and parents away.

When Jesus saw what his friends were doing, he stopped them and said, "Let the children come to me! Children are special people. They are very close to God, and the kingdom of God belongs to people like them. We should all be more like little children."

Jesus smiled at the children, and they smiled back at him. As each boy and girl came forward, he put a hand on each head and said, "God bless you!" And what do you think the children did then? I think they must have been singing and dancing for joy!

GP275102 New Testament

The Little Children and Jesus

(Activity Page)

Let's Talk About the Story

- What did the children think about Jesus? (*He was a kind man.*)
- What did the children say to their parents? (*"Let's go closer."*)
- What did Jesus' friends try to do? (*Shoo the children away.*)
- What did Jesus say about the children? (*"Let them come to me."*)
- What did Jesus do for each boy and girl? (*He blessed them.*)

God Thinks I'm Special

Remind the children that Jesus thought that children were very special people. Pass around a hand mirror. Have each child look into it while you and their classmates say something special about him or her. (Example: "Jason has a nice smile, a good laugh, a kind way of treating people, a soft voice, a talent for sharing or taking turns," etc.) Give the children photocopies of the badge below and let them draw pictures of themselves in the frame. Pin the badges on the children using large safety pins.

  GP275102 New Testament

The Little Children and Jesus

(Craft Page)

Dancing Children

These children are so happy to see Jesus that they dance in a circle for joy!

Materials needed: photocopies of this craft page, crayons, scissors, glue

Directions: Let the children color and cut out the two patterns along the bold lines. Then they can roll and glue them together as shown with the pictures on the outside.

Palm Sunday

(Zechariah 9:9, Matthew 21:1–11)

A Parade in Jerusalem

(You might use the craft on page 34 to illustrate this story. Show a palm branch if available.)

Long before Jesus was born, a prophet named Zechariah told the people, "Your Savior will come into Jerusalem riding on a little donkey, and everyone will shout for joy." And what Zechariah said came true.

Many years later, Jesus and his friends were walking along on the road to Jerusalem. They were coming to the big city to celebrate the Feast of the Passover. From a long way off, they could see the shining white walls of the temple and people crowding into the city.

Just before they got to the huge gate to the city, Jesus stopped his friends and said, "I need a donkey to ride on. Borrow one for me." So away they went and found a donkey. They spread a bright blanket over the little animal, and Jesus climbed on its back. "Now let's go into the city," he said.

When people heard that Jesus was coming, there was great excitement in Jerusalem. "Who's coming?" some people asked. "It's Jesus, the preacher from Nazareth," other people answered.

Crowds of people ran out to meet Jesus and ran alongside the donkey, shouting, "Hosanna! Hosanna!" which means "Hooray! Hooray!" Some others called, "God bless you, Jesus!" and "Praise God in highest heaven for our Savior!" Some of them put their coats down in the road for the donkey to walk on, and many of them broke branches off of palm trees to wave like tall, green flags. "Welcome, Jesus, welcome!" they sang. And that's why we remember that exciting day and call it Palm Sunday.

Some other people who were watching the parade didn't know who the man was, riding through the gates of Jerusalem on a donkey, smiling at everybody. But Jesus' friends knew who he was: He was the Savior that Zechariah had told about long ago—the Savior, riding into Jerusalem on a little donkey.

GP275102 New Testament

Palm Sunday
(Activity Page)

Let's Talk About the Story

- What did Zechariah say the Savior would do someday? *(ride into Jerusalem on a donkey)*

- What did Jesus ask his friends to borrow for him? *(a donkey)*

- What does "Hosanna" mean? *(hooray)*

- Did everyone know who Jesus was? *(No.)*

- What did some people lay in the road? *(their coats)*

- What did some people wave at Jesus? *(palm branches)*

Let's Have a Parade!

When the children carry these colorful butterflies in a parade, everyone will take notice! Ahead of class time, roll 9" x 12" sheets of bright construction paper into 12"-long narrow cylinders and tape them closed. Cut butterflies from construction paper using the pattern below and print HOSANNA! on each. Cut three 25" bright streamers for each child and tape them together. Let the children help assemble the pieces as shown below and then carry them in a joyous Palm Sunday procession—outdoors, if possible. How about singing and ringing bells, too?

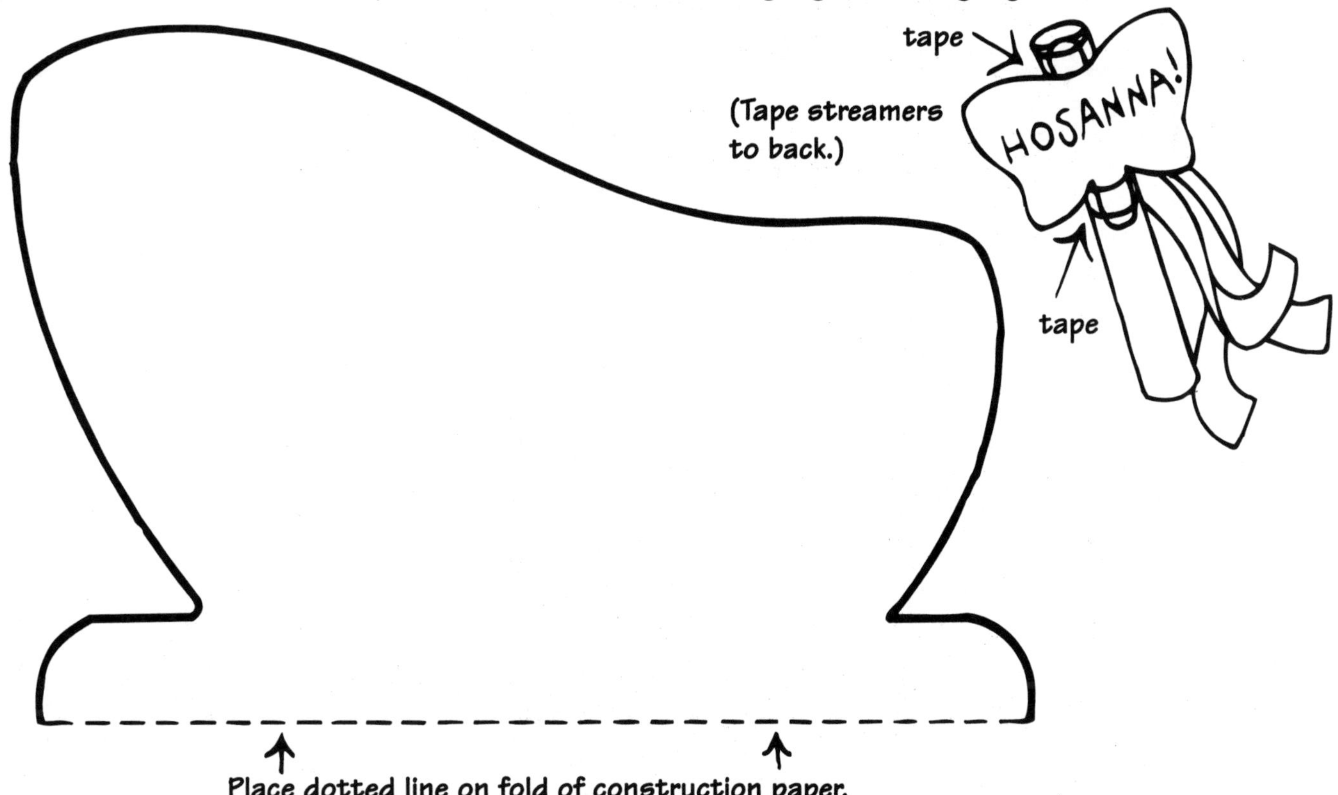

Place dotted line on fold of construction paper.

Palm Sunday

(Craft Page)

The Lucky Little Donkey

This donkey was lucky enough to carry Jesus on his back. He even sports a nice little saddle blanket!

Materials needed: photocopies of this craft page, 1¾" x 2½" rectangles of bright-colored cloth, crayons, scissors, glue

Directions: Have the children color their donkeys and cut them out along the bold lines. (Note that one cut line extends over the head to the back.) Tell them to fold on the dotted lines and glue as shown. Next, they fold the cloth and glue it on the donkey's back.

Overlap and glue.

Fold cloth. Place on donkey's back.

GP275102 New Testament

The Last Supper

(Luke 22:7–38)

The Good-bye Supper

(You might use the craft on page 37 to illustrate your story.)

Jesus and his friends, the disciples, had come to Jerusalem to celebrate the Feast of the Passover. His friends were feeling very happy. They had watched as Jesus rode into the city on a little donkey while big crowds of people danced and sang and waved palm branches. Now they were looking forward to having a special supper together.

In a big upstairs room, they all gathered around a table. It was filled with special things to eat for the holy day. The friends ate and drank and talked together happily. At first, nobody noticed how quiet Jesus was.

At the end of the meal, Jesus said, "I've been looking forward to eating this supper with you. And now I have to tell you that this is the last supper we will eat together." The disciples suddenly got very sad and quiet. What could Jesus mean?

"Very soon," said Jesus, "I'm going to be with my Father in heaven. This is a good-bye supper, so I want to do something special tonight."

Then Jesus picked up a loaf of bread that was lying on the table. He broke it into pieces so everyone could have a share. He blessed it, and then he said, "From now on, whenever you eat bread together, remember me."

Then he took a glass of wine, blessed it, and shared it with his friends. He said, "Here's something else that will help you remember me. Whenever you drink wine together, remember me and this last good-bye supper."

The disciples were sad, but they ate the bread and drank the wine together. They promised Jesus that they would never forget him and the things he taught them.

Even now, 2,000 years later, people still get together and remember Jesus and the good-bye supper. They eat the bread and remember. They drink the wine (or the grape juice), and they remember. Let's all remember Jesus with love!

The Last Supper

(Activity Page)

Let's Talk About the Story

- What did Jesus and the disciples do to celebrate Passover? *(They had a special supper together.)*

- What news did Jesus tell his friends that made them sad and quiet? *(This was their last supper together.)*

- What did Jesus do with the bread and the wine? *(He blessed them and shared them with the disciples.)*

- What did Jesus want his friends to do whenever they ate bread and drank wine together? *(remember him)*

Reminders

Ahead of time, make a photocopy of the "Jesus loves me" note below for each child and glue it to a 3" x 3" square of felt. Tell the children that at the Last Supper, Jesus gave his friends reminders—things to remember him by. Show the children the pictures below and ask them what each object might remind us to do. Give a "Jesus loves me" note to each child. Let the children suggest places they might keep them.

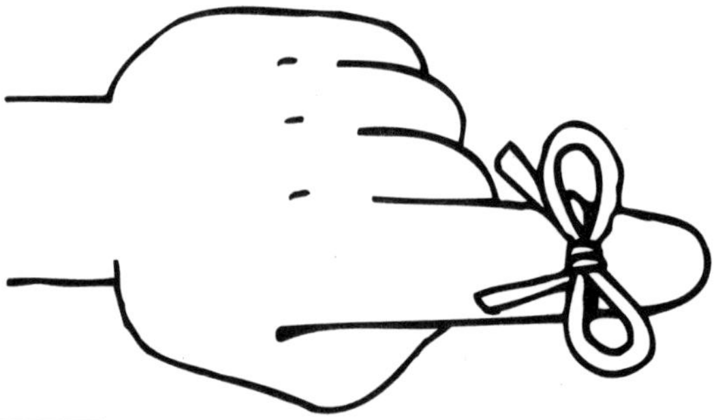

 GP275102 New Testament

The Last Supper 

(Craft Page)

The Remember-Me Supper

This craft gives the children a glimpse of that important Last Supper table in Jerusalem. It also illustrates the sacrament of Communion.

Materials needed: photocopies of this craft page, one 4" x 8" sheet of colored construction paper per child, crayons, scissors, glue

Directions: Print "Remember Me" along one edge of each sheet of construction paper. Let the children color the bread and cup, cut them out along the bold lines, fold on the dotted lines, and glue them to their construction paper "tables" as shown.

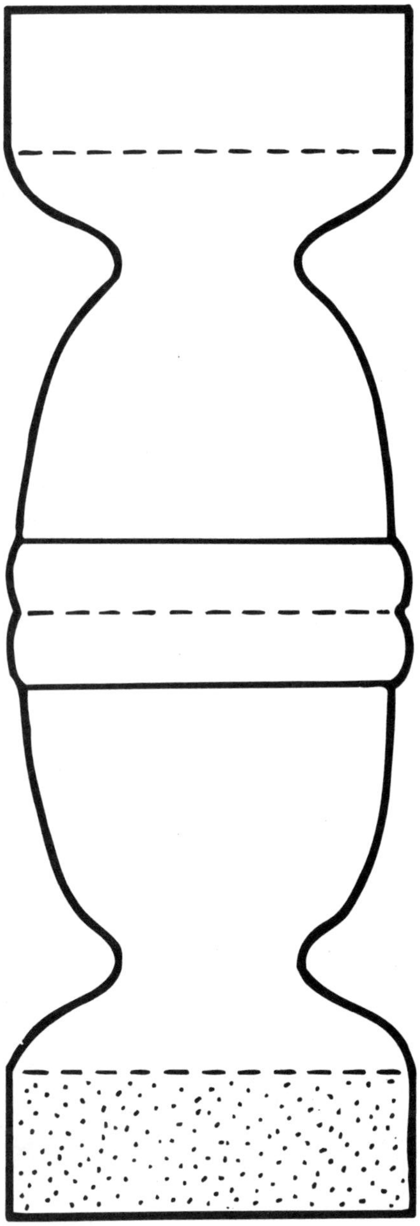

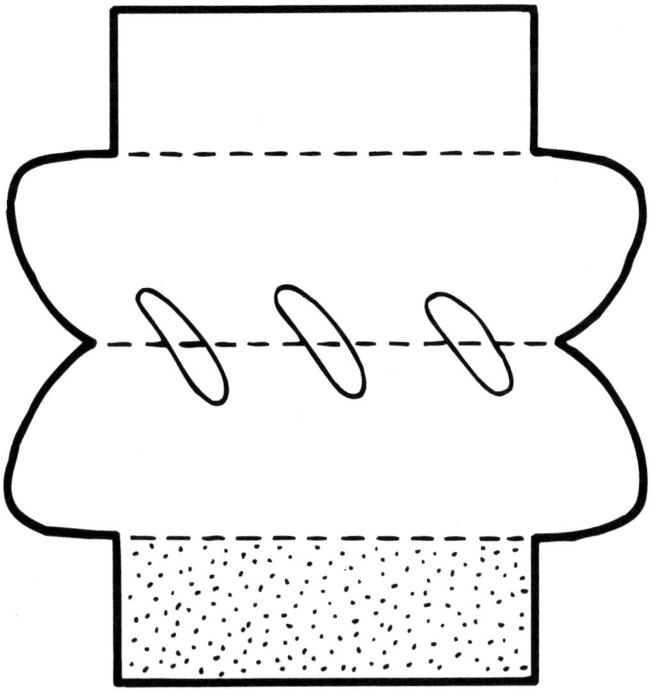

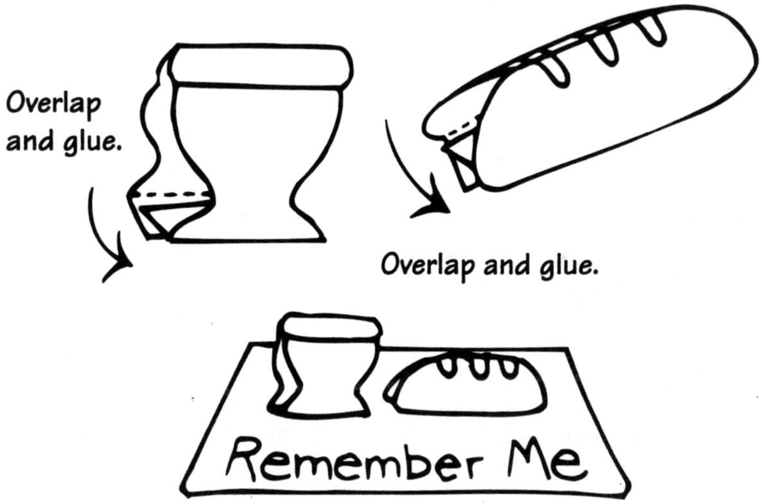

Easter

(John 14:1–4, 20:1–23; Matthew 20)

Easter Promises

(Show the children an Easter egg as you begin this story.)

There's a good reason why we think about eggs at Easter—because they help us think about new life. Sometimes, new life comes out of an egg like this: a brand-new baby chick! On Easter, we remember some promises Jesus made to us. Here's a story about the Easter promises:

After Jesus died on the cross, his friends put his body in a tomb that had a huge rock for a door. And they thought, "Jesus is gone forever."

But three days later, Jesus' friend, Mary Magdalene, went to visit the tomb and found a strange thing—the rock door had been opened! Mary ran to get two of the disciples. They came back with her and looked inside the tomb. And they saw that Jesus' body was gone! "Well, Jesus said he would rise to life after three days," they said. Could it be true? They went home to think about it. Mary Magdalene stayed outside of the tomb and cried because she missed Jesus so much.

All of a sudden, Mary Magdalene heard a little rustling behind her. When she turned around, a man was standing there.

"Who are you looking for?" the man asked. And then he said her name: "Mary."

She knew that voice! Mary wiped the tears from her eyes and said, "Jesus!" Then Jesus told her, "Go and tell my friends that I have risen to new life, just as I promised."

Mary ran all the way to tell the disciples. At first, they didn't believe her. But then they said, "Jesus made us a promise. He said that he would rise to new life so he could go and prepare a place for us in heaven. Jesus wouldn't break a promise!"

Later, when the disciples had gathered together, Jesus came to them and made another promise. He said, "I will be with you always." And those are promises Jesus makes to us, too—that we'll have new life, and that he will be with us forever. And those are the promises we celebrate at Easter time.

 GP275102 New Testament

Easter

(Fingerplay)

Let's Talk About the Story

- What did the disciples discover when they looked in the tomb? *(Jesus' body was missing.)*

- What did Mary do after the disciples left? *(She stayed by the tomb.)*

- Who was the man behind Mary? *(Jesus)*

- What two promises did Jesus make? *(that he would rise and prepare us a place in heaven; that he would be with us always)*

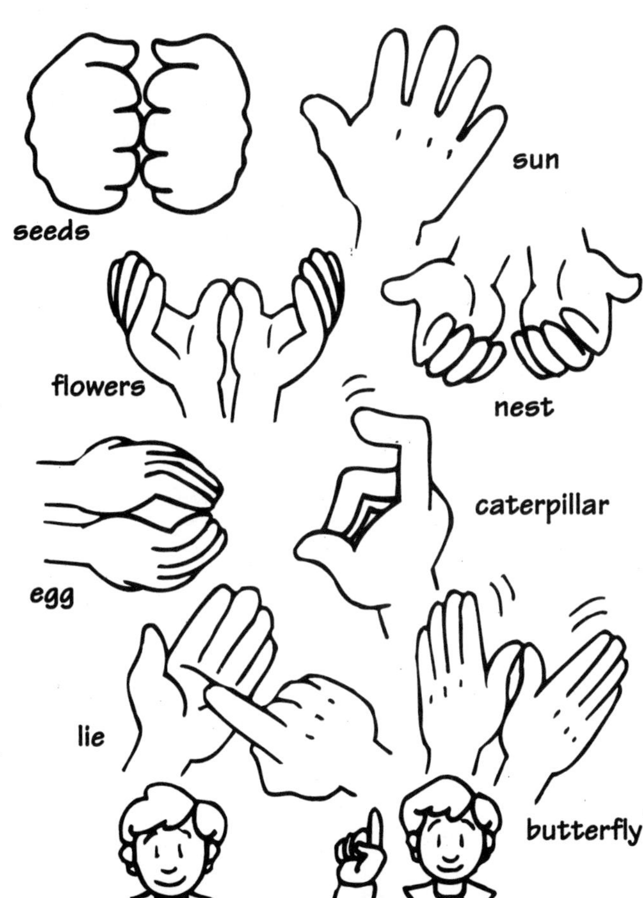

Easter Secrets Fingerplay

(Use the gestures shown for each underlined word.)

Little <u>seeds</u> are sleeping,
Underneath the snow.
And when the warm spring <u>sun</u> comes out,
A hundred <u>flowers</u> will grow!

In a cozy farmyard <u>nest</u>,
Three shiny white <u>eggs</u> hide.
The eggs are holding secrets—
There are baby chicks inside!

A <u>caterpillar</u> makes a bed,
And there he'll safely <u>lie</u>.
Until one day he'll waken,
And come out a <u>butterfly</u>!

In spring, God sends the warming <u>sun</u>,
And signs of hope and <u>love</u>,
And Easter's promise of new life
In heaven up <u>above</u>.

Easter

(Craft Page)

Hooray for New Life!

The children will have fun making this lovely and meaningful Easter decoration for use at home.

Materials needed: photocopies of this craft page, crayons, scissors, glue

Directions: Let the children color the craft and cut it out along the bold lines. They can roll and glue as shown.

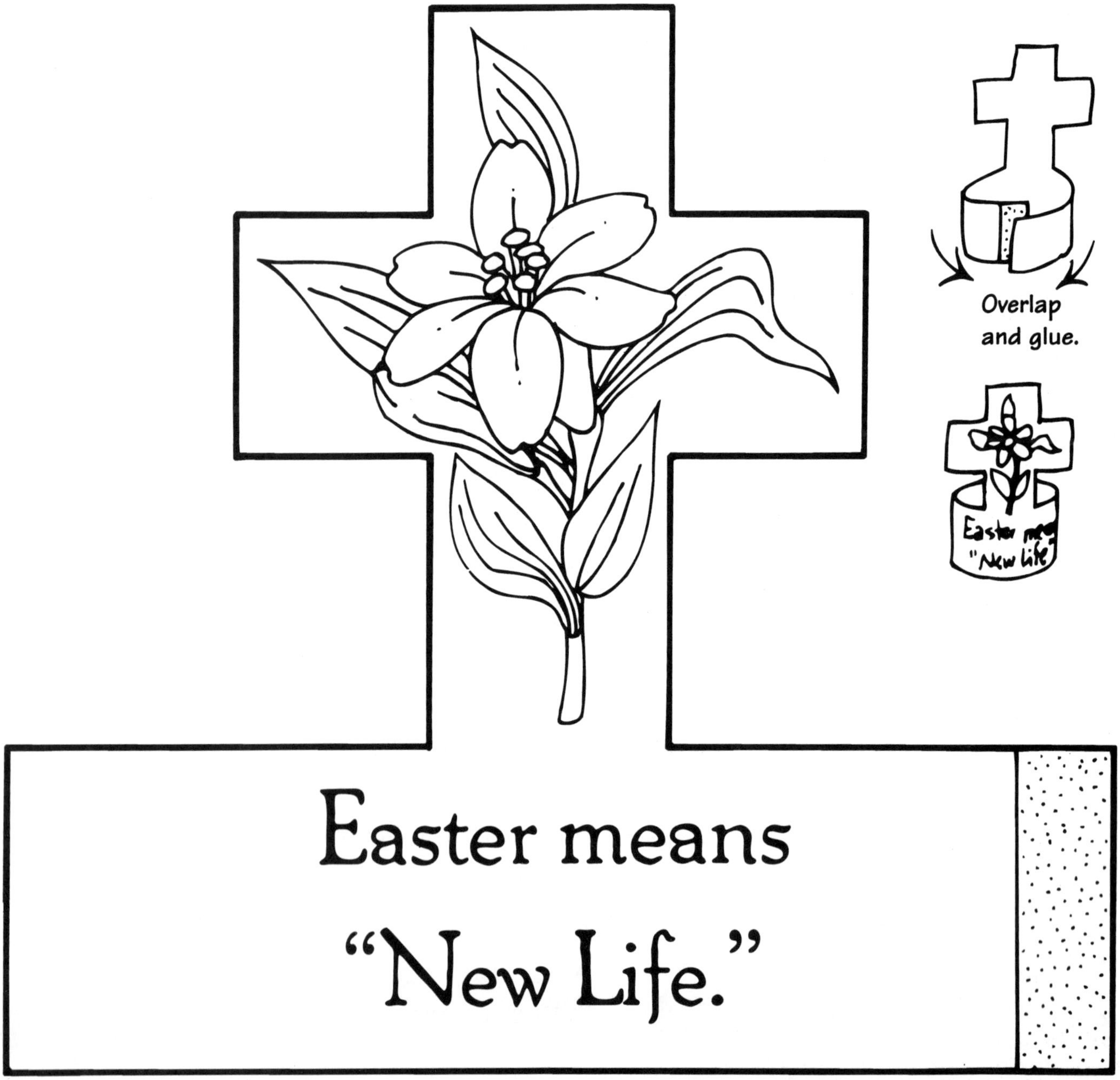

Overlap and glue.

Easter means "New Life."

GP275102 New Testament

Pentecost

(Acts 2)

The Wind and the Fire

(Say the words in parentheses to help the children participate.)

Before Jesus rose to new life, he told the disciples to stay in Jerusalem. He said they would get a gift there. So his disciples waited in Jerusalem. Now, a holiday called Pentecost was coming, and the disciples were all gathered together. Peter was in charge. But no one there was sure how to carry on the work that Jesus had started.

Peter said, "Friends, we all know what Jesus wanted us to do. He wanted us to carry the Good News of God's love to everyone. Even though we're not sure what to do, we need to start making some plans."

While they were talking things over, some wonderful things began to happen. They heard a big wind *(make a sound like the wind)* roaring in the sky above them, and the sound came thundering through the windows and around the walls of the house where they were gathered. Then, as they looked at one another, a beautiful little light, like a fire, appeared above everyone's head. *(Make your hands into a little flame shape, above your head.)* While they were still wondering at that, everybody there began to talk about God in strange languages.

By this time, people out in the streets were running to the house and peeking in the windows to see what was happening. "Listen to the wind!" people said. "Look at the fire! These folks are all from Galilee, but they're speaking languages from a lot of different countries. Something strange is happening in there!"

Since a big crowd had gathered, Peter must have thought it was a good time to start preaching, right there. And that's what he did. "Jesus promised us that the Holy Spirit would be with us, and that's what's happening here!" he said. "Now you can see that Jesus really was the Messiah, the Son of God."

After that, more and more people heard the Good News and became Christians, like Peter and the other friends of Jesus. They shared everything they had with one another. They worshipped and prayed together. They gave thanks and praised God every day. And whenever they ate bread and drank wine together, they thought of what Jesus had told them: "Remember me." This was the beginning of the Christian church.

  GP275102 New Testament

Pentecost

(Activity Page)

Let's Talk About the Story

- Why did Jesus' friends have a meeting? *(to make plans about preaching the Good News to everyone)*
- Who was in charge of the meeting? *(Peter)*
- What wonderful thing did they hear? *(a big wind)*
- What wonderful thing did they see? *(light over each person's head)*
- What wonderful thing did they do? *(They spoke in many languages.)*
- What did Peter do when the big crowd gathered? *(preached)*

Good News Greeting Card

The children can take Peter's Good News home to their families! Ahead of time, photocopy the box below for each child and glue it inside a 9" x 12" sheet of light-colored construction paper. Let the children decorate the front of their greeting cards with crayons or stickers.

© Grace Publications   GP275102 New Testament

Pentecost
(Craft Page)

Wind-and-Fire Windsock

When completed, this flame-covered windsock can hang outdoors and wave in the wind!

Materials needed: photocopies of this craft page, crayons, bright-colored ribbons or streamers, hole punch, string, glue

Directions: Let the children color the craft and cut it out along the bold lines. As shown, help the children glue streamers along the bottom, then roll up their windsocks and glue. Punch two holes at the top of each windsock and help each child insert a 20" loop of string through the holes as shown.

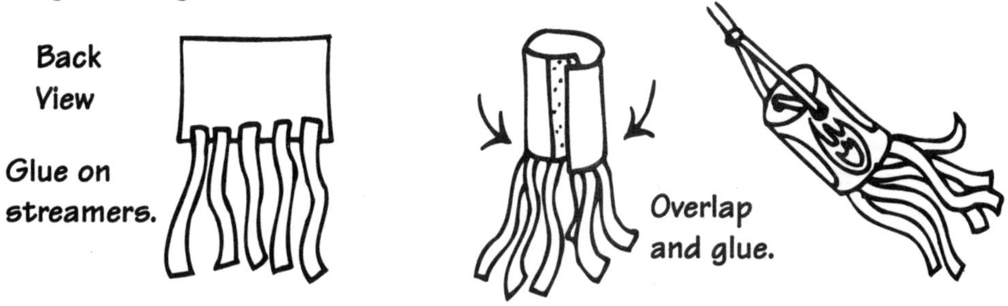

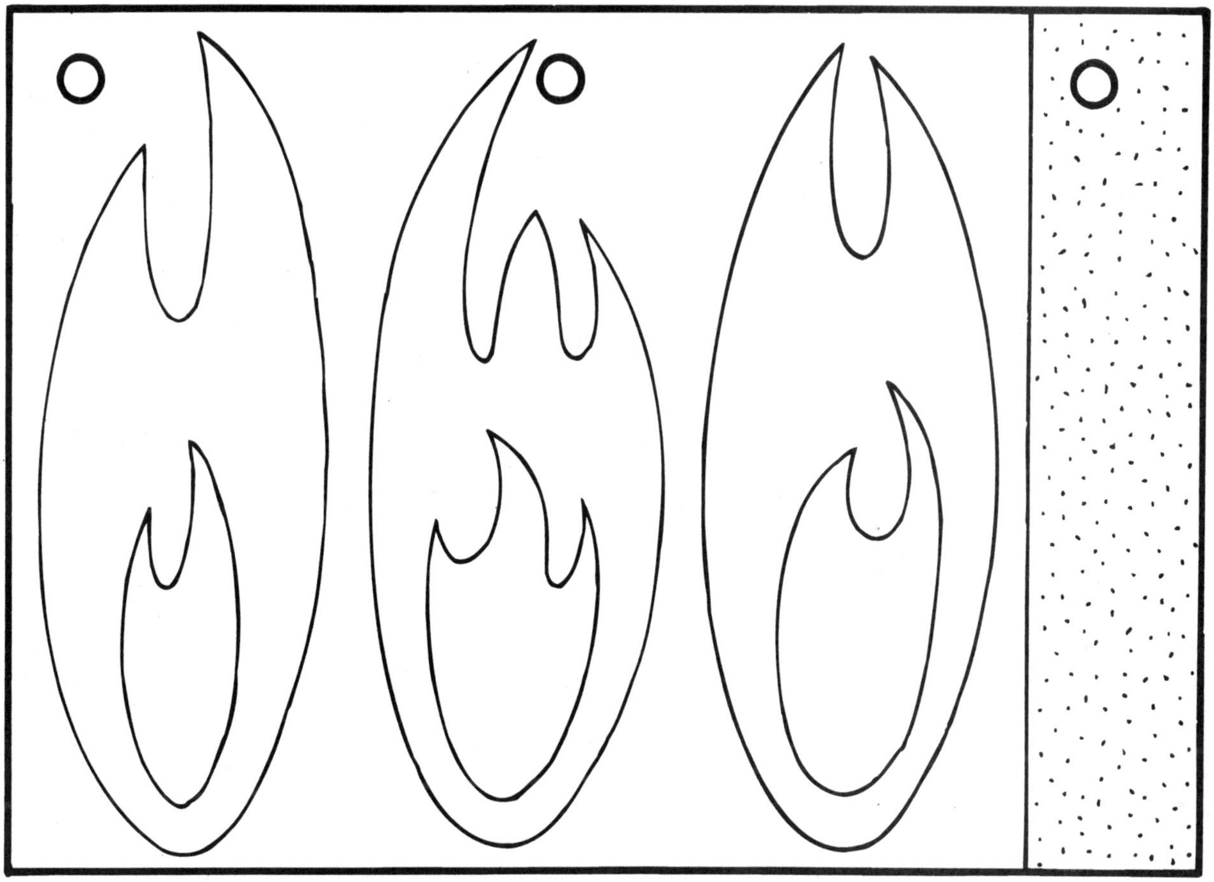

GP275102 New Testament

Paul's Shipwreck

(Acts 27–28:1–10)

Shipwreck!

(You might use the craft on page 46 to illustrate this story.)

A good man named Paul traveled everywhere, by land and by sea, to tell everyone about Jesus and his promises for new life. One day, he got on a ship that was going across the sea to Rome.

For a while, everything was just fine. Then a big storm came up. The sailors tried to sail the boat to shore, but the wind kept blowing it out to sea. Day after day, the waves grew higher. The sailors were so scared, they couldn't even eat. But Paul told them, "Don't be afraid! God sent an angel to me last night to tell me our ship would be wrecked, but we would all be safe." Paul believed God, but the sailors didn't.

That night, the storm grew worse, and they got ready to get into the lifeboats. "No!" said Paul. "God wants us to stay on the ship, and then we'll be safe." Then he told them, "You haven't eaten for a long time. Eat some food and you'll feel better." Paul took some bread and said a blessing. The sailors ate, and sure enough, they did feel better. They put down their anchors for the night.

When morning light came, they looked through the fog and rain and saw an island off in the distance. They cut off their anchors, and the ship began to move toward the land. But when they were almost there, the front of the ship hit some rocks and stuck there. The wind and the huge waves pounded the ship against the rocks, and it began to break apart.

Paul and all the sailors jumped overboard into the sea. Some of them swam through the high waves, and some held onto broken pieces of wood from the ship so they would float. And just as the angel had said, they were all saved.

The people of the island came out and met them on the shore. They built a big fire to warm the shipwrecked sailors and gave them food to eat. Paul must have been thinking, "I knew God would keep us safe. If God says something, it is always true."

 GP275102 New Testament

Paul's Shipwreck 

(Activity Page)

Let's Talk About the Story

- Why was Paul traveling everywhere? *(to tell people about Jesus and his promises of new life)*

- What happened when the ship was at sea? *(A big storm came up.)*

- What did Paul tell the frightened sailors? *("Don't be afraid. God said we would be safe.")*

- What did they see in the morning? *(an island)*

- What did the people of the island do for Paul and the sailors? *(built a fire to warm them and gave them food)*

- What did Paul say about trusting God? *(If God says something, it is always true.)*

Blow Paul's Ship to the Island!

Make at least four photocopies of the boat and sail patterns below before introducing this activity. Then, using a coffee mug for a pattern, cut out circles from blue construction paper. Next, cut out the ships and sails. Using the tip of a pencil, poke holes where indicated. Tape the ends of each boat together. Assemble as shown using 6" pipe cleaners. Tape over each stem on the bottom of the blue paper. Provide a smooth tabletop and place a box on a chair at one end to represent the island. Using drinking straws, the children take turns blowing Paul's little boat across the table and into the box. (Older children might want to have boat races.)

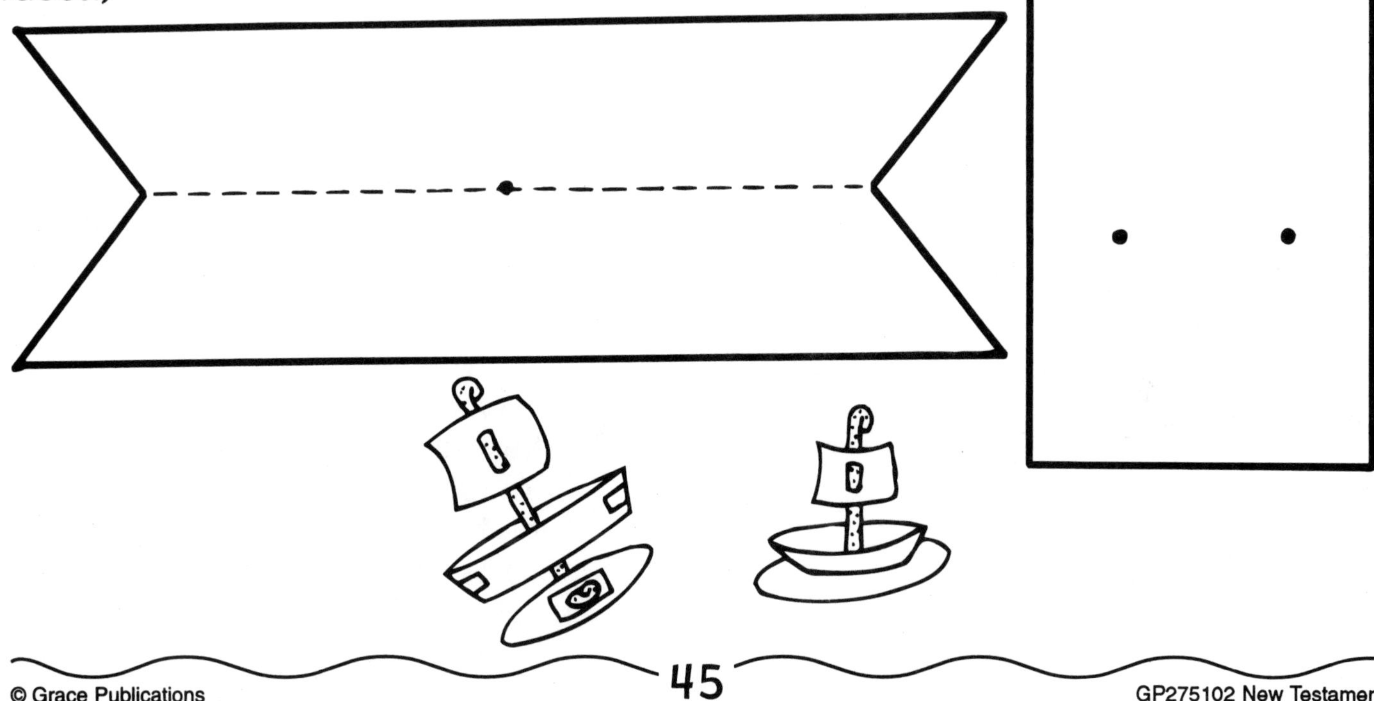

GP275102 New Testament

Paul's Shipwreck

(Craft Page)

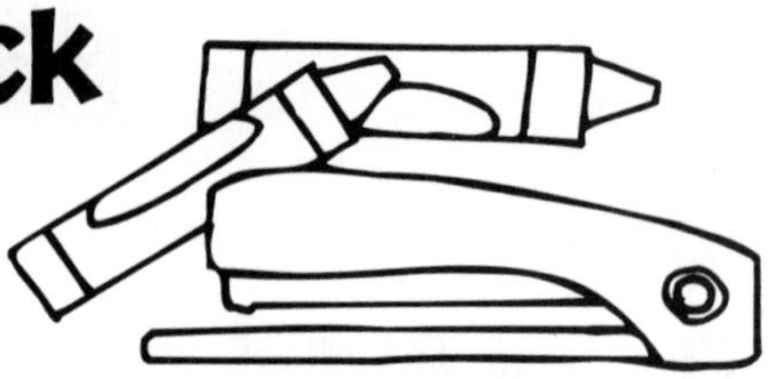

Put Paul in the Ship

The children can place Paul aboard and carry this ship home to retell the story.

Materials needed: photocopies of this craft page, crayons, scissors, staples

Directions: Let the children color the ship and Paul and cut them out along the bold lines. Then they fold their ships on the dotted lines and staple them as shown. Last, they can insert Paul.

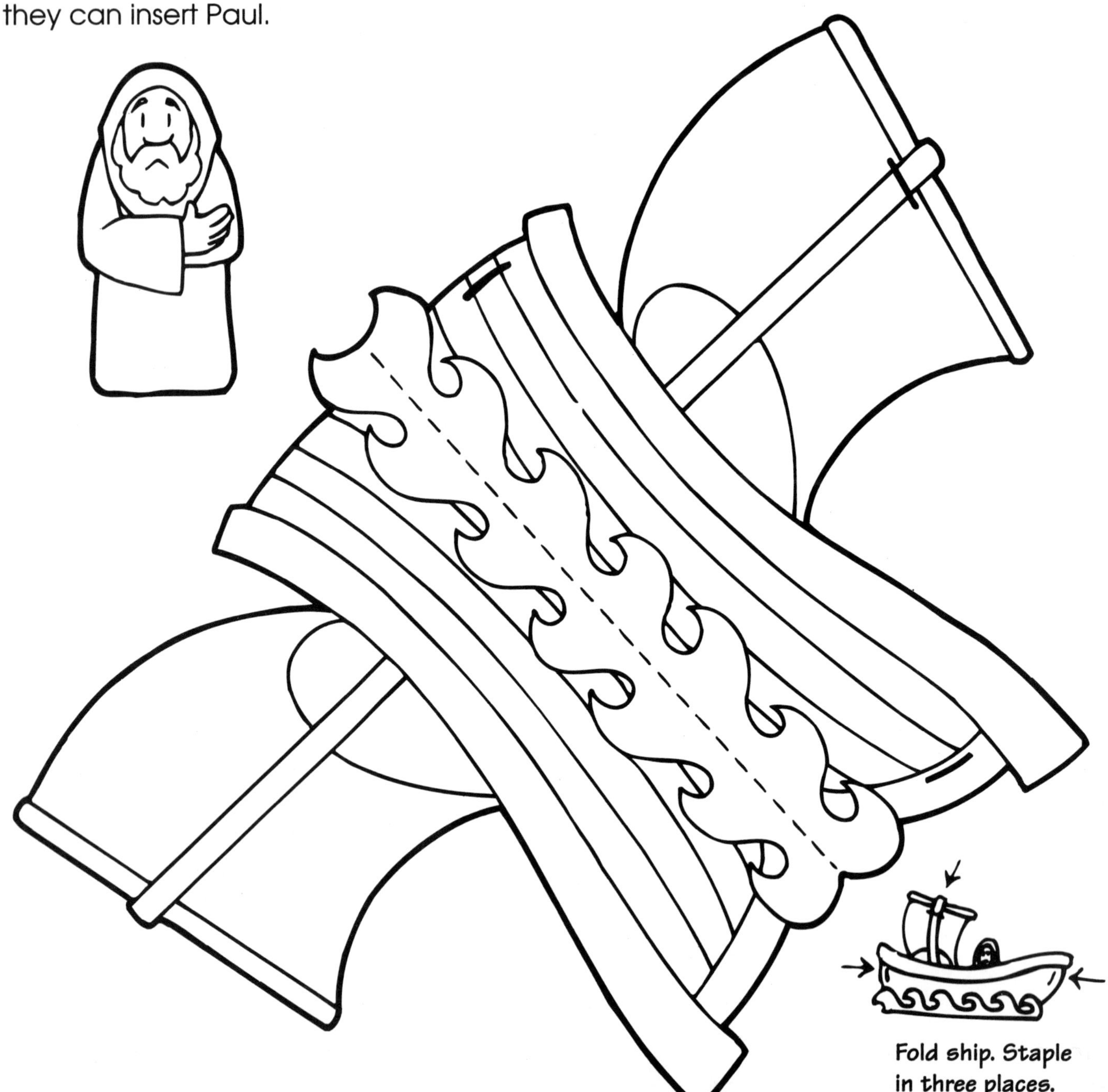

Fold ship. Staple in three places.

The Love Chapter

(1 Corinthians 13)

Love Is the Best Thing of All

(Begin by printing LOVE in bold letters on a large sheet of paper.)

Remember the story about Paul traveling across the sea and escaping from the shipwreck?

Well, Paul kept right on traveling all around, telling people about God's love. And every place he went, he stopped to write letters to his Christian friends. The most famous letter he ever wrote was all about love. Here's what Paul wrote:

"God gives each of us wonderful gifts, but shall I tell you what is the best gift of all? It's <u>love</u>!

"Do you know what love is like? I'll tell you. If I were smart enough to speak hundreds of languages, but didn't show love to others, I'd just be making a lot of noise. If I were so smart that I knew everything about the world, and even knew what was going to happen tomorrow, but didn't show love to my neighbors, I wouldn't be such a great person.

"If I had so much faith that I could move a mountain just by talking to it, but didn't show love to my family and friends, I wouldn't really be so wonderful and special.

"How can you show love to others? You can be always patient and kind. You'll never be jealous of other people, and never brag about yourself, and you'll never be selfish or rude. If you want to show love to others, you'll never be grouchy, and you'll never tell them lies. You'll be a friend, no matter what."

Then Paul told his friends: "God sees into our hearts. Let him look into all of our hearts and see the best thing of all: love."

The Love Chapter

(Craft Page)

Let's Talk About the Story

- What did Paul write to his friends about? *(love)*

- What are some ways Paul says you can show love? *(Be patient and kind; never be jealous, selfish, or rude; never be grouchy; always tell the truth.)*

- What did Paul say was the best of all God's gifts? *(love)*

Love Is the Best Gift of All

Here's a colorful reminder of Paul's good and important words!

Materials needed: photocopies of this craft page, crayons, scissors, glue

Directions: Have the children color the craft. Next, they cut it out, roll it into a cylinder, and glue as shown.